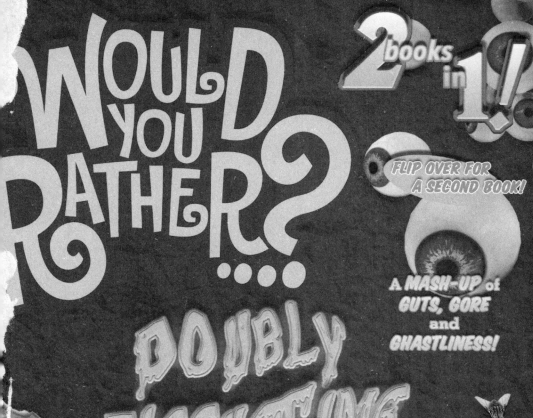

WOULD YOU RATHER?....

DOUBLY DISGUSTING

2 books in 1!

FLIP OVER FOR A SECOND BOOK!

A **MASH-UP** of **GUTS, GORE** and **GHASTLINESS!**

Justin Heimberg & David Gomberg

A Would You Rather...? DOUBLE FEATURE

Published by Seven Footer Press
165 Madison Avenue
Suite 201
New York, NY 10016
First Printing, July 2015
10 9 8 7 6 5 4 3 2
Manufactured in Mayfield, Pennsylvania, 07/15
© Copyright Justin Heimberg and David Gomberg, 2015
All Rights Reserved

Design by Thomas Schirtz

ISBN 978-1-939158-67-3

www.sevenfooterpress.com

Table of Contents
Gross Out

Table of Contents
Doubly Disgusting

HOW TO USE THIS BOOK

1. Sit around with a bunch of friends.

2. Read a question from the book out loud and talk about it.

   You won't believe some of the stuff you'll come up with as you think about which choice to make.

3. Everybody must choose! That's the whole point. It forces you to really think about the options.

4. Once everyone has chosen, move on to the next question.

It's that simple. We have provided a few things to think about for each question, but don't stop there. Much of the fun comes from imagining the different ways your choice will affect your life. You may want to grab a pencil, as sometimes, you will get to fill in the blank with the name of someone you know or other information. Other times, you will make up your own questions, keep score of who chose what, and more! Enough jibber-jabber. It's time to enter the demented world of *Would You Rather...?*

Flippin' the Script!

You might notice as you thumb through this book, things become more than a little bit "twisted." Don't worry. You're not going crazy. This isn't just a book. It's two books. Twice the fun. Twice the gross. Twice the awesome. We've taken the best of two of the most-est grossest books and even sprinkled in some new silly spice into the mix. Here's how to handle it. When you're sick of—or from— the first half of this book, you can flip it over for some even greater "gross-out" questions. Or, if you're a master gymnast, just flip yourself over instead and do a handstand, in which case you won't need to spend any energy turning the book around. Or, if you are truly dedicated, elect to have an experimental surgery in Switzerland where they rotate one of your eyes 180 degrees so that one of your eyes sees the world upside-down. Then, it is just a matter of keeping the correct eye shut at the appropriate time. These are all reasonable solutions. You can read the whole first half before moving on to the second, or go back and forth. As always with *Would You Rather...*, it's up to you. You must choose!

CHAPTER ONE

DISGUSTING!

You asked for disgusting, and you got it. Concerning all things nasty, vile, and just plain gross, these sick questions will hit you like a hailstorm of boogers. Each question offers two possible fates, each delightfully more disgusting than the next. Choose wisely.

Would you rather...

step in dog doo every fifth step you take

OR

get hit with bird poop every thirty seconds no matter where you are, even inside?

Would you rather...

produce 100 times the amount of saliva you currently produce

OR

produce 100 times the boogers you currently produce?

YOU MUST CHOOSE!

Would you rather...

sleep nightly in a bed of worms

OR

bathe daily in a tub filled with lobsters?

Would you rather...

retrieve a marble at the bottom of a barrel of thumbtacks

OR

at the bottom of a barrel of cockroaches?

Take a vote!

Number of people who voted for choice #1:.........

Number of people who voted for choice #2:.........

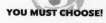

YOU MUST CHOOSE!

WOULD YOU RATHER...LICK AN ICE CREAM CONE COVERED IN ANTS

OR EAT A HOT DOG SMOTHERED IN CATERPILLAR GUTS?

Would you rather...

eat a peanut butter and jellyfish sandwich

OR

a ham and toe cheese (the gunk between your toes) sandwich?

Would you rather...

toss a handful of walnuts into your mouth, only to discover that they were actually beetles

OR

chew on a piece of bubble gum, only to discover that you were actually chewing on a live baby squid?

YOU MUST CHOOSE!

Would you rather...

gargle a mouthful of dog slobber

OR

eat a cat's hairball?

Take a vote!

Number of people who voted for **choice #1**:.........

Number of people who voted for **choice #2**:.........

YOU MUST CHOOSE!

Would you rather...

only be able to drink out of rain puddles

OR

be fed regurgitated food by your mom like mother birds feed their chicks?

Would you rather...

have nose hair that touches the ground

OR

armpit hair that grows around your arms like ivy?

YOU MUST CHOOSE!

Would you rather...

have a permanent paper cut between your fingers

OR

a permanent canker sore in your mouth?

Who chose what and why...

Name _____ Choice _____

Why _____

Name _____ Choice _____

Why _____

Name _____ Choice _____

Why _____

YOU MUST CHOOSE!

Would you rather...

sneeze moths

OR

cough up tiny frogs?

Would you rather...

eat salmon-flavored ice cream with salmon chunks **OR** bubble gum ice cream full of already chewed gum wads?

broccoli-flavored ice cream **OR** Centipedes N' Cream?

Ground Beef Sherbet **OR** Lima Bean Sorbet?

What's the most disgusting flavor you can come up with?

YOU MUST CHOOSE!

Would you rather...

eat potato-bug salad

OR

consume a jelly donut where the jelly is snot?

Reasons **1st** *choice* is better

....
....
....
....

Reasons **2nd** *choice* is better

....
....
....
....

YOU MUST CHOOSE!

18

WOULD YOU RATHER... HAVE TO SLEEP EVERY NIGHT HANGING UPSIDE DOWN LIKE A BAT

OR EAT OUT OF A TROUGH WITH THE REST OF YOUR FAMILY LIKE A GROUP OF PIGS?

Disgusting!

Would you rather...

have a runny nose that won't quit for a month

OR

a bloody nose that won't quit for a day?

Who chose what and why...

Name _____ Choice _____

Why _____

Name _____ Choice _____

Why _____

Name _____ Choice _____

Why _____

YOU MUST CHOOSE!

Would you rather...

lick an ashtray **OR** a pig's lips?

the floor of your school cafeteria **OR** the floor of a barber shop?

the bottom of your friend's foot **OR** the top of a termite mound?

Would you rather...

have to drink a warm glass of sweat each morning **OR** have to eat a larva grub each morning rather than a daily vitamin?

YOU MUST CHOOSE!

Make Your Own "DISGUSTING" Question!
Make up **two choices** that are **equally disgusting!**

Would you rather...

_____

_____

OR

_____ ?

_____

Who chose what and why...

Name _____ Choice _____

Why _____

Name _____ Choice _____

Why _____

Name _____ Choice _____

Why _____

WOULD YOU RATHER... WEAR A WASP NEST AS A HAT

OR WEAR A KING COBRA AS A TIE?

Would you rather...

sneeze through your butt

OR

fart through your nose?

Would you rather...

get a zit on your tongue **OR** your eyeball?

in your nostril **OR** right in the center of your forehead?

a zit the size of a marble on the tip of your nose **OR**
the size of a golf ball on the bottom of your chin?

YOU MUST CHOOSE!

Would you rather...

have to brush your hair with a used toilet scrub brush

OR

use Super Glue as shampoo?

Would you rather...

your eyelids were permanently flipped inside out

OR

be permanently cross-eyed?

YOU MUST CHOOSE!

WOULD YOU RATHER...
HAVE BOTH EYES ON ONE SIDE OF YOUR FACE LIKE A FLOUNDER

OR HAVE ELEPHANT TUSKS?

Would you rather...

have a mobile plan that offers unlimited texting

OR

a special pass that grants permission for unlimited farting?

YOU MUST CHOOSE!

CHAPTER TWO

BAD LUCK

Unlucky you. It seems that the fates have decided to complicate your life in a most bizarre way. You are to suffer a strange curse that will change your life forever (and not for the better). Well, at least you'll have some say in the matter, since you get to choose between two equally horrific choices.

Would you rather...

always talk like you do when you're holding your nose

OR

talk like you do when you're gargling water?

Would you rather...

have a permanent wind blowing in your face

OR

permanent fingerpaint on your hands?

YOU MUST CHOOSE!

Would you rather...

have corduroy skin

OR

have suction cups all over your body like an octopus?

YOU MUST CHOOSE!

Would you rather...

have to clean yourself like a cat

OR

have to use a litter box like a cat?

Would you rather...

blink 100 times per minute

OR

be unable to ever shut your eyes?

YOU MUST CHOOSE!

Would you rather...

share your house with three of your teachers

OR

have to go to school seven days a week?

Reasons *1st choice* is better

....
....
....
....

Reasons *2nd choice* is better

....
....
....
....

YOU MUST CHOOSE!

Would you rather...

have a horse's tail **OR** a baboon's butt?

a pig's snout for a nose **OR** a rooster's wattle under your chin (the fleshy piece of skin hanging under the beak)?

reindeer antlers sprouting from the top of your head **OR** a rhino horn jutting out from the front of your face?

Would you rather...

talk at six times normal speed

OR

one-third normal speed?

YOU MUST CHOOSE!

Would you rather...

have a crazy straw for an outie belly button

OR

have pipe cleaner hair?

Would you rather...

when passing by people on the street, be compelled to guard them as if playing basketball

OR

feel the urge to stuff acorns in your cheeks like squirrels do?

EXTRA WEIRD!

YOU MUST CHOOSE!

Would you rather...

only be able to eat garnish to survive

OR

only be able to eat food that begins with the letter "y"?

YOU MUST CHOOSE!

Would you rather...

sleep every other hour

OR

every other day?

Who chose what and why...

Name _____ Choice _____

Why _____

Name _____ Choice _____

Why _____

Name _____ Choice _____

Why _____

YOU MUST CHOOSE!

Would you rather...

have a perpetual watch glint shining in your eyes

OR

a constant itch on your back that you can't reach?

Would you rather...

have a belly button that rings like a doorbell when pushed

OR

one that has a Magic 8-Ball readout in it?

YOU MUST CHOOSE!

WOULD YOU RATHER...HAVE THE LETTERS ON YOUR KEYBOARD RANDOMLY CHANGE EVERY DAY

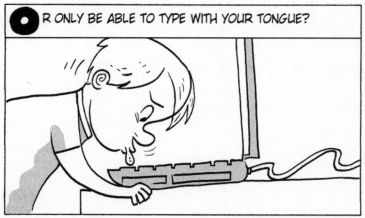

OR ONLY BE ABLE TO TYPE WITH YOUR TONGUE?

Would you rather...

wake up each day with a new hair color and style

OR

a new last name?

Take a vote!

Number of people who voted for **choice #1**:.........

Number of people who voted for **choice #2**:.........

Would you rather...

have the face of an 80-year-old

OR

the face of a 2-year-old?

YOU MUST CHOOSE!

Make Your Own "BAD LUCK" Question!
Make up two choices that are equally weird!

Would you rather...

_ _ _ _ _ _ _ _ _ _ _ _ _ _ _ _ _ _ _ _

_ _ _ _ _ _ _ _ _ _ _ _ _ _ _ _ _ _ _ _

OR

_ _ _ _ _ _ _ _ _ _ _ _ _ _ _ _ _ _ _ _

_ _ _ _ _ _ _ _ _ _ _ _ _ _ _ _ _ _ _ ?

Who chose what and why...

Name _____ Choice _____

Why _____

Name _____ Choice _____

Why _____

Name _____ Choice _____

Why _____

Would you rather...

fart laughing gas

OR

cry chocolate syrup?

Reasons **1ˢᵗ choice** is better

....
....
....
....
....

Reasons **2ⁿᵈ choice** is better

....
....
....
....
....

Would you rather...

have a bed that flips you out to wake you in the morning

OR

one that heats up?

YOU MUST CHOOSE!

Would you rather...

neigh like a horse when you get upset

OR

howl like a coyote when you're excited?

Take a vote!

Number of people who voted for **choice #1**:.........

Number of people who voted for **choice #2**:.........

YOU MUST CHOOSE!

Would you rather...

have to get everywhere by riding a Big Wheel

OR

by using a hippity hop ball?

Who chose what and why...

Name _____ Choice _____

Why _____

Name _____ Choice _____

Why _____

Name _____ Choice _____

Why _____

YOU MUST CHOOSE!

WOULD YOU RATHER... HAVE A BIRD BRIEFLY POP OUT OF YOUR MOUTH AT NOON EACH DAY LIKE A CUCKOO CLOCK

OR LITERALLY BEGIN TO MELT WHEN EXPOSED TO TEMPERATURES OVER 85 DEGREES?

Would you rather...

be raised by dogs **OR** chimps?

be raised by angels **OR** the Harlem Globetrotters?

be raised by 5-year-olds **OR** One Direction?

YOU MUST CHOOSE!

Would you rather...

be unable to distinguish between sinks and toilets

OR

pillows and beehives?

Would you rather...

never be able to save an e-mail

OR

a picture?

YOU MUST CHOOSE!

Would you rather...

have to write without using vowels

OR

without using your hands?

Who chose what and why...

Name _____ Choice _____

Why _____

Name _____ Choice _____

Why _____

Name _____ Choice _____

Why _____

YOU MUST CHOOSE!

Would you... accept a $10,000 check from Donald Trump if you then had to have his hair style for the rest of your life?

Would you rather...

be tethered to your home by a 200-foot cord

OR

become as light as helium when the sun goes down?

YOU MUST CHOOSE!

Would you rather...

all your weight go to your thighs **OR** to your butt?

to your stomach **OR** to your ankles and upper arms?

to your neck **OR** to your forehead?

Who chose what and why...

Name _____ Choice _____

Why _____

Name _____ Choice _____

Why _____

Name _____ Choice _____

Why _____

YOU MUST CHOOSE!

Would you rather...

have an eyelash comb-over

OR

have nose hair that connects from one nostril to the other?

Would you rather...

have to still use a bib **OR** a car seat?

a bottle **OR** diapers?

a stroller **OR** a high chair?

YOU MUST CHOOSE!

Would you rather...

always feel like you do when you eat too much

OR

always feel like you've got to go number one?

Who chose what and why...

Name _____ Choice _____

Why _____

Name _____ Choice _____

Why _____

Name _____ Choice _____

Why _____

YOU MUST CHOOSE!

Would you rather...

only be able to write using the first 13 letters of the alphabet

OR

the last 13? Try it!

A B C D E F G H I J K L M

N O P Q R S T U V W X Y Z

YOU MUST CHOOSE!

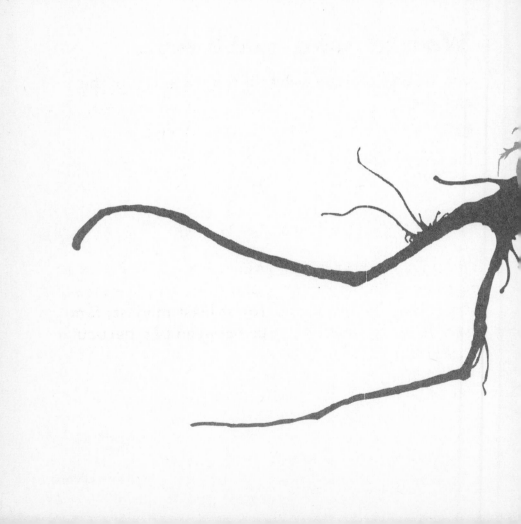

CHAPTER THREE

Your Wildest-ish Dreams

The tides have turned in your favor. You're about to hit the jackpot in the form of a super (or at least super-ish) power or your wildest (or at least mildest) fantasy. Even better, you get a choice between two particular positives.

Would you rather...

have a pencil that magically answers
all math questions correctly

OR

a fielder's mitt that magically catches
all fly balls?

Would you rather...

be able to dry yourself after showering by shaking your
hair like a wet dog

OR

have self-combing hair?

YOU MUST CHOOSE!

Would you rather...

be able to remember every second of your life from the time you were born

OR

not remember anything other than the last day but know precisely what will happen to you in the future?

Reasons **1ˢᵗ choice** is better

....
....
....
....
....

Reasons **2ⁿᵈ choice** is better

....
....
....
....
....

YOU MUST CHOOSE!

WOULD YOU RATHER.. HAVE LADLES FOR HANDS

SOUP

OR TENNIS RACKETS FOR FEET?

Would you rather...

be able to correctly identify the person who farted with 100% accuracy

OR

have the ability to use your snot as Krazy Glue?

Would you rather...

have a visor that can slide in and out of your forehead

OR

have Heelys built into the bottoms of your feet?

YOU MUST CHOOSE!

Would you rather...

have a Nerf lawn

OR

have beanbag bushes?

Take a vote!

Number of people who voted for **choice #1**:.........

Number of people who voted for **choice #2**:.........

YOU MUST CHOOSE!

Would you rather...

have extra eyeballs in the palms of your hands

OR

not?

Would you rather...

your family be secret agents

OR

a world-famous band?

YOU MUST CHOOSE!

WOULD YOU RATHER...
HAVE A THUMB THAT DOUBLES AS A PEZ
DISPENSER

OR BE ABLE TO SPRAY PAINT WITH YOUR MOUTH?

Would you rather...

be able to answer any teacher's question when called on, but only if you used a phony French accent

OR

be able to solve any math problem, but only while barefoot?

Reasons **1st choice** is better

....
....
....
....
....

Reasons **2nd choice** is better

....
....
....
....
....

EXTRA WEIRD!

YOU MUST CHOOSE!

Would you rather...

live in the White House

OR

an amusement park?

Would you... accept the power to be able to fly in exchange for weighing 500 pounds?

YOU MUST CHOOSE!

Would you rather live in a world...

where it rained root beer

OR

where it snowed cheese puffs?

Take a vote!

Number of people who voted for **choice #1**:.........

Number of people who voted for **choice #2**:.........

YOU MUST CHOOSE!

Would you rather...

that babies were born with a mute button

OR

parents were?

Reasons *1st choice* is better

....
....
....
....
....

Reasons *2nd choice* is better

....
....
....
....
....

YOU MUST CHOOSE!

Would you rather...

own a self-making bed

OR

self-folding clothes?

Would you rather...

have the power to instantly thaw frozen food by dropping it down your pants

OR

be able to exterminate roaches by breathing on them?

EXTRA WEIRD!

YOU MUST CHOOSE!

Would you rather...

have a sandpaper tongue

OR

switchblade fingernails?

Would you rather...

be reincarnated as a rabbit

OR

a snake?

YOU MUST CHOOSE!

Would you rather...

your dreams were written by JK Rowling

OR

the writers of *Guardians of the Galaxy*?

Would you rather...

never miss a basketball free throw

OR

be able to dunk any object other than a basketball?

YOU MUST CHOOSE!

Would you rather...

be able to pop popcorn kernels in your closed fist

OR

be able to make real sounds when playing air guitar?

Reasons 1st choice is better

....
....
....
....
....

Reasons 2nd choice is better

....
....
....
....
....

YOU MUST CHOOSE!

Would you rather...

have a daily allowance of 10,000 calories with no weight gain

OR

have the ability to give instant and intense diarrhea to anyone you wish?

Would you rather...

have sugar dandruff

OR

sunflower seed warts?

YOU MUST CHOOSE!

Would you rather...

have perfect aim with spitballs

OR

be able to shoot pencils with your belly fat with the force and accuracy of a bow and arrow?

Reasons **1st choice** is better

....
....
....
....
....

Reasons **2nd choice** is better

....
....
....
....
....

YOU MUST CHOOSE!

Would you rather...

have a panther that obeys your every command and does your bidding

OR

500 hornets that do the same?

YOU MUST CHOOSE!

WOULD YOU RATHER...
HAVE A FROG TONGUE

SNAP!

POPCORN

OR A KANGAROO POUCH?

MATH

Would you rather...

have a panther that obeys your every command and does your bidding

OR

500 hornets that do the same?

YOU MUST CHOOSE!

WOULD YOU RATHER...
HAVE A FROG TONGUE

SNAP!

POPCORN

OR A KANGAROO POUCH?

MATH

B

Would you rather...

get to rename other people whatever you want

OR

rename yourself whatever you want?

Dingwald · The Ambassador · Porp · Chief · President · El Gigante · Chupacabra · Horglemeister · The Boss · Legion · Legolas · King Smelly · Queen Smelly · Prince Smellier · Princess · Warden · Hulk · Dork · Big Guy · Dude · Hottie · Simple Simon · The Pilot · Captain · Porker · Smug Doug · Bud · Art the Fart · Belcher

YOU MUST CHOOSE!

Would you rather...

have the power to know exactly which questions will appear on your tests

OR

get an "A" on any story your write no matter how stupid it is?

Things to consider: What would you write about?

Take a vote!

Number of people who voted for **choice #1**:.........

Number of people who voted for **choice #2**:.........

YOU MUST CHOOSE!

Would you rather...

have nostrils that function as a jetpack

OR

make poops that smell like oranges?

Take a vote!

Number of people who voted for **choice #1**:.........

Number of people who voted for **choice #2**:.........

YOU MUST CHOOSE!

Would you rather...

have LeBron James' dunking skills but permanent, incurable body odor

OR

Tom Brady's passing arm, but permanent, incurable poison ivy on both ankles?

Who chose what and why...

Name _____ Choice _____

Why _____

Name _____ Choice _____

Why _____

Name _____ Choice _____

Why _____

EXTRA WEIRD

YOU MUST CHOOSE!

CHAPTER FOUR

Awfully Unpleasant and Unpleasantly Awful

We're afraid storm clouds have gathered again upon your destiny, perhaps conjured by some wrathful being. For whatever reason, you've been chosen to suffer: something pitifully painful, something excruciatingly embarrassing, something just plain-old bad. But just as you have been chosen, you may choose between two unfortunate fortunes. ☺

Would you rather...

use boiling water eye drops

OR

gargle Tabasco sauce?

Would you rather...

have to wash your mouth out with soap every time you say the word "the"

OR

trip every time you say a word that rhymes with "bat"?

YOU MUST CHOOSE!

Would you rather...

have ten bees fly up your nose

OR

swallow ten live wasps?

Reasons **1st choice** is better

....
....
....
....
....

Reasons **2nd choice** is better

....
....
....
....
....

YOU MUST CHOOSE!

Would you rather...

have to spend a ten hour car ride with the most annoying kid in school

OR

the meanest teacher in school?

Reasons *1st choice* is better

....
....
....
....
....

Reasons *2nd choice* is better

....
....
....
....
....

YOU MUST CHOOSE!

Would you rather...

have to wear the same pair of underwear until you turn 40 years old

OR

be stuck attending nursery school until then?

Take a vote!

Number of people who voted for **choice #1**:.........

Number of people who voted for **choice #2**:.........

YOU MUST CHOOSE!

Would you rather...

have hangnails that are two inches long

OR

have pimples that pop with the sound and force of a firecracker?

Would you rather...

have everyone stick their gum on you when done chewing

OR

have everyone use your shirt as a handkerchief?

YOU MUST CHOOSE!

Would you rather...

have 100 mosquito bites on the inside of your mouth

OR

get poison ivy on the inside of your eyelids?

YOU MUST CHOOSE!

Would you rather...

only be able to drink from water fountains

OR

only be able to eat from vending machines?

Would you rather...

sleep on a pillow covered in porcupine quills

OR

use a blanket of quilted bat wings?

YOU MUST CHOOSE!

Would you rather...

bungee jump off a cliff with the cord attached to your ear

OR

your tongue?

Take a vote!

Number of people who voted for **choice** #1:.........

Number of people who voted for **choice** #2:.........

YOU MUST CHOOSE!

WOULD YOU RATHER...
YOUR LITTLE BROTHER HAVE THE ABILITY TO DIRECT YOUR MOVEMENTS USING A NINTENDO WII CONTROLLER

OR HAVE TO ALWAYS STUFF YOUR PANTS WITH HERMIT CRABS BEFORE LEAVING YOUR HOUSE?

Would you rather...

be the only one the teacher calls on in any of your classes

OR

be responsible for doing the homework for everyone in your classes?

Would you rather...

jump into a pool of piranhas

OR

a pit of rattlesnakes?

YOU MUST CHOOSE!

Would you rather...

always have to dress like an Egyptian pharaoh **OR** a Revolutionary War soldier?

a professional hockey player **OR** a chef?

Fred Flintstone **OR** Buzz Lightyear?

If you had to wear one outfit for the rest of your life, what would it be? ....

YOU MUST CHOOSE!

Would you rather...

be a window washer for the top of the Empire State Building

OR

an underground sewer cleaner?

Take a vote!

Number of people who voted for **choice #1:**.........

Number of people who voted for **choice #2:**.........

YOU MUST CHOOSE!

Would you rather...

watch your dad belly dance

OR

listen to your mom sing in front of the whole school?

Would you rather share your house...

with five pigs **OR** five clowns?

a mime **OR** a crow?

sports announcers who comment on every move you make **OR** 100 St. Bernards?

YOU MUST CHOOSE!

Would you rather...

get caught in an avalanche of boogers

OR

a tidal wave of vomit?

Who chose what and why...

Name _____ Choice _____

Why _____

Name _____ Choice _____

Why _____

Name _____ Choice _____

Why _____

YOU MUST CHOOSE!

WOULD YOU RATHER... BATHE DAILY IN A BATHTUB COATED IN BARNACLES...

OR SLEEP NIGHTLY IN A BED BOLTED TO A SEE-SAW?

Would you rather...

not be allowed to use your hands when you eat

OR

not be allowed to sleep lying down?

YOU MUST CHOOSE!

Would you rather...

wear a shirt full of itching powder

OR

socks filled with angry fire ants?

Would you rather...

have all your eyelashes plucked out

OR

rub rough sandpaper over your recently scraped knee?

YOU MUST CHOOSE!

CHAPTER FIVE

DOUBLY DISGUSTING

Thought things were disgusting enough the first time around? Guess again. That was just practice for what lies ahead on this yellow booger-brick road to Grossville. Bugs? Guts? Scabs and zits and nasty bits? They're all back—this time, bigger, juicier, and smellier. The best you can do is choose the lesser of two evils and salvage a vile "victory".

Would you rather...

have boogers that crawled out of your nose whenever they wanted **OR** boogers the size and shape of dice?

glow-in-the-dark boogers **OR** mood boogers (their color changes depending on your mood)?

helium-filled boogers **OR** boogers that function as Party Snaps (when you toss them on the ground they make small explosion noises)?

YOU MUST CHOOSE!

Would you rather...

drink a glass of ten-month-old moldy milk, feeling every warm chunk as it slides down your throat

OR

eat a cereal bowl of caterpillars with a spoon, feeling the guts forcefully squirt into your mouth as you bite down?

Who chose what and why...

Name _____ Choice _____

Why _____

Name _____ Choice _____

Why _____

Name _____ Choice _____

Why _____

YOU MUST CHOOSE!

Would you rather...

eat 20 sticks of butter

OR

an entire bag of flour?

Who chose what and why...

Name _____ Choice _____

Why _____

Name _____ Choice _____

Why _____

Name _____ Choice _____

Why _____

YOU MUST CHOOSE!

WOULD YOU RATHER... DRINK STRAIGHT FROM A COW'S UDDER

OR EAT A BLOCK OF 20 YEAR OLD MOLDY CHEESE?

Would you rather...

drool creamed spinach

OR

have a pimento (that red thing in olives) in each nostril?

Would you rather...

have a stomach that constantly growls as loud as a lion

OR

a nose that throbs like a human heart?

Reasons *1st choice* is better

....

....

....

Reasons *2nd choice* is better

....

....

....

YOU MUST CHOOSE!

Would you rather...

have to drink a trout milkshake

OR

a meatloaf-flavored sports drink?

Would you rather...

eat a taco full of beetles

OR

eat a cud that has been chewed by a cow for five minutes and then spit out?

YOU MUST CHOOSE!

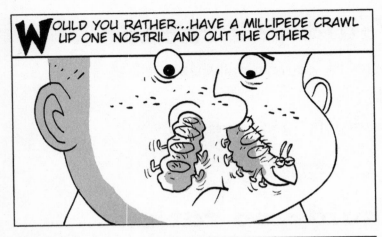

WOULD YOU RATHER...HAVE A MILLIPEDE CRAWL UP ONE NOSTRIL AND OUT THE OTHER

OR HAVE A BABY BAT FLY INTO YOUR MOUTH?

WOULD YOU RATHER...?

2 books in 1!

FLIP OVER FOR A SECOND BOOK!

A *MASH-UP* of *GUTS, GORE* and *GHASTLINESS!*

Gross-Out

Justin Heimberg & David Gomberg

A Would You Rather...? **DOUBLE FEATURE**

Published by Seven Footer Press
165 Madison Avenue
Suite 201
New York, NY 10016
First Printing, July 2015
10 9 8 7 6 5 4 3 2
Manufactured in Mayfield, Pennsylvania, 07/15
© Copyright Justin Heimberg and David Gomberg, 2015
All Rights Reserved

Would You Rather...?® is a registered trademark used under license from Spin Master Ltd.

Design by Thomas Schirtz

ISBN 978-1-939158-67-3

www.sevenfooterpress.com

Table of Contents
Gross Out

Doubly Disgusting
Table of Contents

HOW TO USE THIS BOOK

1. Sit around with a bunch of friends.

2. Read a question from the book out loud and talk about it.

   You won't believe some of the stuff you'll come up with as you think about which choice to make.

3. Everybody must choose! That's the whole point. It forces you to really think about the options.

4. Once everyone has chosen, move on to the next question.

It's that simple. We have provided a few things to think about for some questions, but don't stop there. Much of the fun comes from imagining the different ways your choice will affect your life. You may want to grab a pencil, as sometimes, you will get to fill in the blank with the name of someone you know or other information. Other times, you will make up your own questions, keep score of who chose what, and more! Enough jibber-jabber. It's time to enter the demented world of *Would You Rather...?*

Flippin' the Script!

You might notice as you thumb through this book, things become more than a little bit "twisted." Don't worry. You're not going crazy. This isn't just a book. It's two books. Twice the fun. Twice the gross. Twice the awesome. We've taken the best of two of the most-est grossest books and even sprinkled in some new silly spice into the mix. Here's how to handle it. When you're sick of—or from— the first half of this book, you can flip it over for some "Doubly Disgusting" questions. Or, if you're a master gymnast, just flip yourself over instead and do a handstand, in which case you won't need to spend any energy turning the book around. Or, if you are truly dedicated, elect to have an experimental surgery in Switzerland where they rotate one of your eyes 180 degrees so that one of your eyes sees the world upside-down. Then, it is just a matter of keeping the correct eye shut at the appropriate time. These are all reasonable solutions. You can read the whole first half before moving on to the second, or go back and forth. As always with *Would You Rather...*, it's up to you. You must choose!

CHAPTER ONE

GROSS!

For reasons beyond your understanding, you are about to engage in some seriously enGROSSing activities. That fascination you have with vomit, vermin, boogers, and bugs is about to come back to haunt you. You wanted gross, you got it. On the bright side, you are given a choice between two possible fates, each delightfully more disgusting than the next.

Would you rather...

swallow five live cockroaches

OR

bathe for ten minutes in a bathtub full of octopi?

Would you rather...

have to eat a frozen snotsicle

OR

a roadkill hot dog?

YOU MUST CHOOSE!

WOULD YOU RATHER...HAVE TO WASH YOUR FACE EVERYDAY IN A HEAVILY POPULATED BIRD BATH

OR HAVE TO BRUSH YOUR TEETH EACH DAY WITH TWO YEAR OLD NACHO CHEESE?

GROSS!

Would you rather...

stick your tongue in the hole of a bowling ball at the local bowling alley

OR

blow your nose using a stranger's used tissue?

Reasons *1st choice* is better
....
....
....
....
....

Reasons *2nd choice* is better
....
....
....
....
....

YOU MUST CHOOSE!

Would you rather...

eat a meal made from food found in the back of a garbage truck

OR

sleep a night in the back of a garbage truck?

Reasons **1st** *choice* is better

....
....
....
....

Reasons **2nd** *choice* is better

....
....
....
....

YOU MUST CHOOSE!

Fill in the Blank!

Would you rather...

have to kiss _____ for 20 seconds
(insert animal)

OR

gargle with_____ for 20 seconds?
(insert liquid)

YOU MUST CHOOSE!

Would you rather...

have night crawler worms come out whenever you sneeze

OR

bees fly out when you cough?

Would you rather...

wear clothes made out of sopping wet seaweed

OR

sleep in a bed of raw ground beef?

YOU MUST CHOOSE!

Would you rather...

drink the pus from 50 popped white-head pimples

OR

take a shower in camel spit?

Take a vote!

Number of people who voted for **choice #1**:.........

Number of people who voted for **choice #2**:.........

YOU MUST CHOOSE!

Would you rather...

permanently share your bedroom with:

1,000 mosquitoes **OR** 5 boa constrictors?

a gassy Bigfoot **OR** an elephant with allergies?

25 black widow spiders **OR** 3 pits filled with quicksand?

YOU MUST CHOOSE!

WOULD YOU RATHER...
NEVER BE ABLE TO OPEN
UP YOUR MOUTH WHEN
THROWING UP

OR HAVE YOUR NOSTRILS
AND LIPS SEAL UP WHEN
YOU SNEEZE?

AT CHOO!

Would you rather...

slurp a bowl of soup made from a broth flavored with used retainers

OR

eat a grilled chicken breast that was marinated in a hobo's armpit sweat?

YOU MUST CHOOSE!

Would you rather...

eat an olive where the pimento is replaced with a slug

OR

a chocolate chip cookie where the "chips" are dead flies?

Who chose what and why...

Name _____ Choice _____

Why _____

Name _____ Choice _____

Why _____

Name _____ Choice _____

Why _____

YOU MUST CHOOSE!

15

Would you rather...

eat a grilled cheese covered in maggots

OR

a caramel apple rolled on the floor of a barber shop?

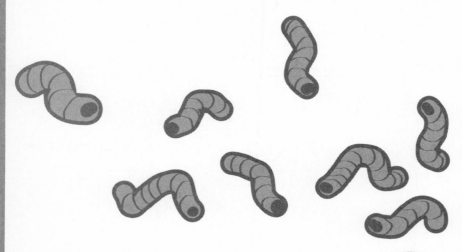

YOU MUST CHOOSE!

Would you rather...

produce poops that wriggle and squirm like snakes upon falling in the toilet

OR

fart to the tune of "You're a Grand Old Flag"?

Would you rather live in a world...

where people sniffed each other like dogs when they met

OR

where they charged each other like rams?

YOU MUST CHOOSE!

Would you rather...

gargle quick-drying cement mouthwash

OR

inhale Krazy glue nasal spray?

Take a vote!

Number of people who voted for **choice #1**:.........

Number of people who voted for **choice #2**:.........

YOU MUST CHOOSE!

Would you rather...

wear a sweater infested with fleas

OR

use a blanket woven from spider webs full of dead bugs?

Would you rather...

have dandelions for hair **OR** your choice of pasta?

dangerous electric wire **OR** centipedes?

tree branches **OR** tentacles?

YOU MUST CHOOSE!

WOULD YOU RATHER... EAT A SUNDAE WITH AN OLIVE FOR A CHERRY AND BROCCOLI INSTEAD OF NUTS

OR A "ZUCCHINI SPLIT" WITH KETCHUP INSTEAD OF HOT FUDGE?

Would you rather...

never be able to bathe/shower

OR

never be able to flush a toilet?

Take a vote!

Number of people who voted for **choice #1**:.........

Number of people who voted for **choice #2**:.........

GROSS!

YOU MUST CHOOSE!

21

Would you rather...

be thrown up on by six giraffes

OR

get farted on by a rhino?

Would you rather...

eat a piece of cake that had a 50% chance of having a dead mouse in the middle

OR

grab and eat a handful of M&M's with one third of those M&M's actually being fish eyes?

YOU MUST CHOOSE!

Would you rather...

vomit purple spray paint **OR** dice?

marbles **OR** lightning bugs?

thumb tacks **OR** a bullet at full speed?

YOU MUST CHOOSE!

Would you rather...

eat a scoop of ice cream out of an old dirty shoe

OR

eat a salad sprinkled with boogers?

Would you rather...

lick your friend's chicken pox

OR

use Tabasco sauce eye drops?

YOU MUST CHOOSE!

Would you rather...

have no furniture in your house

OR

have no toilet in your house?

Take a vote!

Number of people who voted for **choice #1**:.........

Number of people who voted for **choice #2**:.........

GROSS!

YOU MUST CHOOSE!

CHAPTER TWO

YOU'VE BEEN CURSED

For reasons beyond your understanding, you are about to suffer a terrible curse—something that will change your life forever in all sorts of ways. Luckily for you, there is a faint silver lining to this dark cloud. You get to choose between two possible fates.

Would you rather...

have a cow's udder on your stomach

OR

a turkey neck with lots of skin hanging down?

Would you rather...

only be able to hear words spoken by accountants

OR

upon hitting the age of 60, slowly turn into a salmon?

EXTRA WEIRD!

YOU MUST CHOOSE!

Would you rather...

have 2 tongues **OR** 20 toes?

8 nostrils **OR** no nostrils?

4 ears **OR** 4 lips?

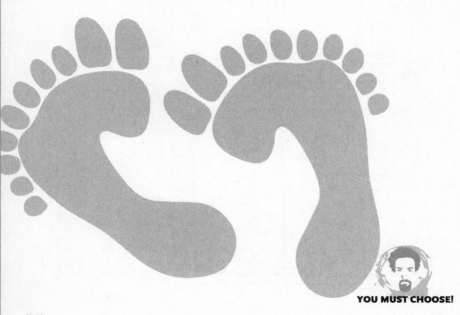

YOU MUST CHOOSE!

Would you rather...

have fingernails that grow at a rate of one inch per minute

OR

have eyebrows that grow at the same rate?
Things to consider: vision problems, sports, picking your nose

Would you rather...

change the first letter of your first name to "V"

OR

change the first letter of your last name to "B"?

YOU MUST CHOOSE!

Would you rather...

have red eyes

OR

glow-in-the-dark veins?

Reasons *1st choice* is better

....
....
....
....
....

Reasons *2nd choice* is better

....
....
....
....
....

YOU MUST CHOOSE!

Would you rather...

gain 50 pounds between the hours of 11AM and 2PM every day, returning to your normal weight again after 2PM

OR

instead of getting tan in sunlight, become plaid?

Things to think about: lunchroom sumo

EXTRA WEIRD!

YOU MUST CHOOSE!

Would you rather...

suck in air with the force of a vacuum when yawning

OR

have blow-dryer strength farts?

Take a vote!

Number of people who voted for choice #1:.........

Number of people who voted for choice #2:.........

YOU MUST CHOOSE!

Would you rather...

have corkscrew thumbnails **OR** jolly rancher toenails?

skateboards for feet **OR** paintbrushes for hands?

Stegosaurus spikes along your spine **OR** an anteater snout?

YOU MUST CHOOSE!

WOULD YOU RATHER...HAVE THE PHYSIQUE OF A BABY, BUT ENLARGED

OR HAVE VELCRO BODY HAIR?

Would you rather...

have an echo that mocks you

OR

a shadow that does?

Would you rather...

only be able to open your eyes 1/8th of an inch

OR

only be able to open your mouth 1/8th of an inch?

YOU MUST CHOOSE!

WOULD YOU RATHER...HAVE FISH FOR HANDS

OR MOPS FOR FEET?

Would you rather...

only be able to wear yellow clothing

OR

have to use a flounder for a wallet?

Would you rather...

have saltwater saliva

OR

grape Gatorade sweat?

YOU MUST CHOOSE!

WOULD YOU RATHER...ALWAYS HAVE TO WEAR AN NFL REFEREE UNIFORM

OR A WIZARD'S ROBE?

Would you rather...

have pockets filled with an infinite supply of Gummi Bears but be incapable of speaking when not wearing a headband and matching wristbands

OR

have near-perfect knowledge of computer programming but on Fridays become convinced you are a glass of orange juice and desperately struggle not to spill yourself?

EXTRA WEIRD!

YOU MUST CHOOSE!

Would you rather...

fart the sound of a tuba

OR

hiccup the sound of a harmonica?

Reasons *1st choice* is better

....
....
....
....
....

Reasons *2nd choice* is better

....
....
....
....
....

YOU MUST CHOOSE!

Would you rather...

only gain weight on the top half of your body

OR

only gain weight on the left side of your body?

Take a vote!

Number of people who voted for **choice #1**:.........

Number of people who voted for **choice #2**:.........

YOU MUST CHOOSE!

Would you rather...

walk through all doorways as if you were in the middle of an intense limbo competition

OR

have a strange desire to always make a hula hoop motion whenever you're in the presence of your school principal?

EXTRA WEIRD!

YOU MUST CHOOSE!

WOULD YOU RATHER...HAVE BENDY STRAWS FOR HAIR

OR NEWSPAPER FOR SKIN?

WOULD YOU RATHER...
LIVE IN A GIANT VERSION OF A HAMSTER CAGE

OR IN A GIANT ANT FARM?

Would you rather...

have all your eye blinks last 10 seconds

OR

have all your yawns last 2 hours?

Who chose what and why...

Name _____ Choice _____

Why _____

Name _____ Choice _____

Why _____

Name _____ Choice _____

Why _____

YOU MUST CHOOSE!

Would you rather...

have moles that wander all over your face and body

OR

have miniature ivory walrus tusks on your face?

Reasons *1st choice* is better
....
....
....
....
....

Reasons *2nd choice* is better
....
....
....
....
....

YOU MUST CHOOSE!

Would you rather always have to wear...

clothes in the style of a 2 year old **OR** an 80 year old?

a stethoscope in your ears **OR** a scuba mask and snorkel?

a full New York Mets uniform **OR** a lettuce eye patch?

YOU MUST CHOOSE!

Would you rather...

have an Adam's apple the size of a coconut

OR

big toes the size of light bulbs?

Take a vote!

Number of people who voted for **choice #1**:.........

Number of people who voted for **choice #2**:.........

YOU MUST CHOOSE!

Would you rather...

have to answer your teacher's questions by rapping your answers

OR

by charades?

Would you rather live in a world without...

soap **OR** pizza?

telephones **OR** sports?

pants **OR** the Internet?

YOU MUST CHOOSE!

POWERS AND FANTASIES

Good news! Your luck has turned. You must have eaten all your vegetables or done something right, because the fates are smiling upon you. You are about to be blessed with a magical superpower to rival Superman, Spiderman, and Iron Man. Even better, you have a say in the matter. You get to choose between two options.

Would you rather...

have the power to shoot dental floss from your fingertips

OR

A1 sauce from your eyes?

Would you rather...

be able to blow gum bubbles capable of lifting you into the air like a hot air balloon

OR

have the power to make any food taste like any other food?

YOU MUST CHOOSE!

Would you rather...

have Wii controls that work for real people in front of you (voodoo style)

OR

have every fortune in your fortune cookies become true?

Reasons **1st choice** is better

....

....

....

....

Reasons **2nd choice** is better

....

....

....

....

YOU MUST CHOOSE!

WOULD YOU RATHER...HAVE A HEAD THAT REFLECTS LIGHT LIKE A DISCO PARTY BALL

OR PUFF UP LIKE A BLOWFISH WHEN YOU SENSE DANGER?

Would you rather...

have a Disney Channel musical based on your life

OR

have Domino's name a new type of pizza after you?
Things to consider: What would you name that pizza? What would be on it?

Would you rather...

have multiple lives like in a video game

OR

be able to fast forward life?

YOU MUST CHOOSE!

Would you rather...

be able to able to move and control with your mind: baseball bats

OR

animal bats?

Who chose what and why...

Name _____ Choice _____

Why _____

Name _____ Choice _____

Why _____

Name _____ Choice _____

Why _____

YOU MUST CHOOSE!

WOULD YOU RATHER...HAVE A MINIATURE GOLF COURSE LAWN

OR AN AIR HOCKEY DINNER TABLE?

Would you rather...

have caramel ear wax

OR

hot fudge snot?

YOU MUST CHOOSE!

Would you rather...

win Rock Paper Scissors 90% of the time

OR

never drop a football pass?

Would you rather...

have the power to spray a super stinky musk from scent glands on your butt like a skunk

OR

the ability to surround yourself with a cloud of ink like a squid?

YOU MUST CHOOSE!

Would you rather...

have hair that can harden into a helmet at your command

OR

hair that can shoot out in defense like a porcupine's quills?

Reason 1st choice is better	Reason 2nd choice is better
....	....
....	....
....	....
....	....
....	....

YOU MUST CHOOSE!

WOULD YOU RATHER...HAVE RETRACTABLE CLAWS

OR DREADLOCKS YOU CAN CONTROL?

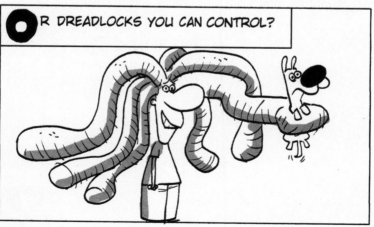

Would you rather never get...

a zit **OR** a stomach ache?

embarrassed **OR** lonely?

a bad grade in school **OR** a bad hair day?

Would you rather...

be able to cool soup to a perfect temperature with merely one blow

OR

be able to neaten sloppy joes by concentrating hard?

YOU MUST CHOOSE!

Make Your Own "Powers" Question!

Would you rather have the power to...

_____

OR

_____?

Who chose what and why...

Name _____ Choice _____

Why _____

Name _____ Choice _____

Why _____

Name _____ Choice _____

Why _____

YOU MUST CHOOSE!

Would you rather...

be able to download songs from iTunes directly into your head

OR

store memories on a laptop computer so they can be watched later?

YOU MUST CHOOSE!

Would you rather...

be able to cause lactose intolerance in people by shaking hands with them

OR

be capable of causing motion sickness in people by singing to them?

Reasons *1st choice* is better

....
....
....
....

Reasons *2nd choice* is better

....
....
....
....

EXTRA WEIRD!

YOU MUST CHOOSE!

Would you rather...

have a toothbrush built into your index finger

OR

a hair brush built into the palm of your hand?

YOU MUST CHOOSE!

Would you rather...

be able to spit globs of phlegm 50 feet with 100% accuracy

OR

have the power to summon background singers at any moment by snapping your fingers?

Would you rather...

drool Pepsi

OR

have rose-scented sweat?

YOU MUST CHOOSE!

Would you rather...

speak fluent Spanish

OR

fluent Pig-Latin?

Would you rather...

have a light saber-like steak knife

OR

have an X-wing Starfighter-shaped car?

YOU MUST CHOOSE!

Would you rather live in a world...

where all foods that were bad for you became good for you

OR

where all arguments with your parents were settled with dodgeball contests?

Take a vote!

Number of people who voted for **choice #1**:.........

Number of people who voted for **choice #2**:.........

YOU MUST CHOOSE!

Would you rather...

be able to levitate one inch off the ground

OR

teleport one inch forward?

Who chose what and why...

Name _____ Choice _____

Why _____

Name _____ Choice _____

Why _____

Name _____ Choice _____

Why _____

YOU MUST CHOOSE!

Would you rather...

be able to inflate your muscles to look strong, but have no actual exceptional strength

OR

be extremely strong, but have the body of a 90 year old?

Who chose what and why...

Name _____ Choice _____

Why _____

Name _____ Choice _____

Why _____

Name _____ Choice _____

Why _____

YOU MUST CHOOSE!

CHAPTER FOUR

COOL AND UNUSUAL PUNISHMENTS

Uh oh. You must have done something wrong again. Seems that the fates have decided that you must suffer a horrible experience—a painful challenge, an embarrassing moment, or something else horrific, disgusting, or just generally unpleasant. ☺

Would you rather...

find out that all of your moments in front of a mirror in the past week have been secretly filmed and will be shown to your school during an assembly

OR

that all of your conversations with friends for the past week have been recorded and will be broadcast on your local radio?

Reasons **1st choice** is better

....
....
....
....

Reasons **2nd choice** is better

....
....
....
....

YOU MUST CHOOSE!

WOULD YOU RATHER...HAVE TO WEAR CLOTHES FIVE SIZES TOO SMALL

OR HAVE TO WEAR ARTICLES OF CLOTHING ON A DIFFERENT PART OF THE BODY THAN THEY WERE INTENDED FOR?

Would you rather...

brush your teeth and gums with steel wool

OR

get a mud mask facial using mud from a pig pen?

Take a vote!

Number of people who voted for **choice #1**:.........

Number of people who voted for **choice #2**:.........

YOU MUST CHOOSE!

Would you rather...

only be able to get around by skipping **OR** galloping?

doing the crabwalk **OR** pogo stick?

by riding a unicycle **OR** by being carried by others?

YOU MUST CHOOSE!

Would you rather...

have to dress identically to your teacher for a week

OR

identically to your mother for a week?

Who chose what and why...

Name _____ Choice _____

Why _____

Name _____ Choice _____

Why _____

Name _____ Choice _____

Why _____

YOU MUST CHOOSE!

WOULD YOU RATHER...FIGHT 3 POSSESSED LAWN MOWERS

OR THE CHARACTERS FROM SPONGEBOB SQUAREPANTS?

Would you rather...

sharpen your index finger in a pencil sharpener

OR

stick your tongue in a pot of boiling water?

What are the 5 most painful things that ever happened to you?

_____

_____

_____

_____

YOU MUST CHOOSE!

Would you rather...

slide down a Slip 'N Slide covered in horse manure

OR

dive into a pool of tuna juice and stay in for 30 minutes?

YOU MUST CHOOSE!

Would you rather...

have to keep 20 mosquitoes in your mouth for ten minutes

OR

take a bath for ten minutes in a tub with a poisonous jellyfish?

Take a vote!

Number of people who voted for **choice #1**:.........

Number of people who voted for **choice #2**:.........

YOU MUST CHOOSE!

Would you rather...

experience a 24-hour atomic wedgie

OR

a 24-hour noogie?

Would you rather...

have a severe allergy to TV **OR** the telephone?

to soap **OR** to paper?

to anyone named John **OR** to the letter "Z"?

YOU MUST CHOOSE!

Would you rather be completely convinced...

that your shadow is out to get you **OR** that your blanket is?

that your belly button is sinking deeper and deeper into your body and will eventually leave a hole through your entire body **OR** that your hair is trying to fly away?

that your uncle is Bigfoot **OR** that the remote control is a baby?

EXTRA WEIRD!

YOU MUST CHOOSE!

WOULD YOU RATHER...EAT A STICK OF COTTON CANDY ENTIRELY MADE FROM BELLY BUTTON LINT

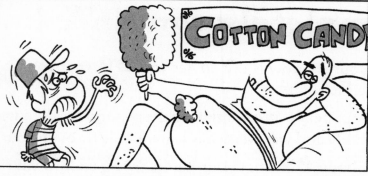

OR DRINK A MILKSHAKE MADE FROM ST. BERNARD SLOBBER?

Would you rather...

see the world in X-box 360 graphic quality

OR

hear all conversations like you were on a cell phone with spotty reception?

Reason **1st** *choice* is better

....
....
....
....
....

Reason **2nd** *choice* is better

....
....
....
....

YOU MUST CHOOSE!

WOULD YOU RATHER...PLAY 30 MINUTES OF CONTINUOUS DODGE BALL AGAINST PEYTON MANNING?

OR WRESTLE JOHN CENA FOR TWO MINUTES?

WOULD YOU RATHER...HAVE EYELASHES THAT GROW AT A RATE OF ONE INCH PER MINUTE

OR HAVE HOT FUDGE PERPETUALLY DRIPPING FROM YOUR NOSTRILS?

Would you rather battle...

the Power Rangers **OR** the Teenage Mutant Ninja Turtles?

a rabid Clifford the Big Red Dog **OR** ten Grovers?

a rhino **OR** all 43 Presidents of the United States?

YOU MUST CHOOSE!

Would you rather...

stick your tongue in a lobster's claw

OR

dive headfirst into a thorn bush?

Would you rather...

lick a cube of dry ice

OR

have a sip of boiling water?

YOU MUST CHOOSE!

CHAPTER FIVE

GROSSER THAN GROSS!

Just when you thought it was safe to eat comes another chapter about the downright dirty and disgusting.
Once again, you are given a choice between two possible fates, each more ridiculously revolting than the next. So what exactly is grosser than gross? You're about to find out.

Would you rather...

produce helium-filled poops **OR** grenade poops (they'll explode in ten seconds)?

perfectly cubed poops **OR** pyramid poops?

poops that fade away in two minutes **OR** poops that change color depending on your mood?

YOU MUST CHOOSE!

Would you rather...

have scent glands on the bottom of your feet

OR

have barnacles all over your body?

Take a vote!

Number of people who voted for **choice #1**:.........
Number of people who voted for **choice #2**:.........

YOU MUST CHOOSE!

WOULD YOU RATHER... EAT A HAMBURGER WITH A "SECRET SAUCE" THAT IS EAR WAX MIXED WITH MAYONNAISE

OR FRENCH FRIES THAT WERE DEEP FRIED IN SWEAT?